CHRISTOPHER PRAYERS FOR TODAY

Other Christopher Books

Add Meaning to Your Life
How to Be a Leader
Now Is the Time
To Light a Candle

CHRISTOPHER PRAYERS FOR TODAY

Richard Armstrong
Director of The Christophers

Introduction by James Keller

PAULIST PRESS
New York / Paramus / Toronto

Designed and illustrated by John Flemming.

Copyright © 1972 by The Christophers, Inc.

Library of Congress
Catalog Card Number: 72-86745

ISBN 0-8091-1735-5

Published by Paulist Press
Editorial Office: 1865 Broadway, N.Y., N.Y. 10023
Business Office: 400 Sette Drive, Paramus, N.J. 07652

Printed and bound in the
United States of America

TABLE OF CONTENTS

INTRODUCTION

"Pray without ceasing" was the advice of the Apostle Paul to the newly founded Christian community in Thessalonika, in present-day Greece.

Paul was a realist who knew that ordinary people had neither the time nor inclination to devote long periods to contemplation. His meaning was: "Pray whenever you can. In short, hurried bursts, if necessary. But if you are to be followers of Christ, and co-workers in the saving of the world, you must be men and women of prayer."

His instructions to us are no different today. Technology may have put us in danger of "future shock," but the need to get beyond our own littleness, apathy or trivial concerns is still present.

This latest Christopher publication urges you to "pray without ceasing," not only for your personal wants, but also for a world that is suffering from a hunger that only God's word and actions can remedy.

The prayers included here are just a beginning. They are to help you find your own occasions for prayer . . . in the eyes of a child . . . waiting for a stop light . . . putting a letter in the mail box . . . in a moment of exultation or defeat . . . in a lover's embrace or after a stinging conflict . . . on a crowded street or utterly alone . . . in the kitchen, office or assembly line.

Prayer should always be intensely personal, but it can discover an exciting new dimension when it is also communal. As much as you can, join with others —in the family, in prayer groups, in church or at some other gathering. No special equipment is necessary. "When two or three are gathered together in My name, there am I in the midst of them." (Matthew 18:20)

A few suggestions:

* Be spontaneous in communicating with God. Formulas are helpful and even necessary, but using your own words adds a freshness.

* Recognize in prayer a bond that unites you with all the world's people, separated by language, power blocs, ethnic and religious diversity.

* Keep trying. Good intentions are not enough. Self-discipline is required for anyone to set aside even a short, regular time each day.

* Remind yourself that you are always in the divine Presence.

* Use the Bible, especially the words and actions of Jesus in the Gospels, for your starting point. The daily newspaper, radio or TV reports will give you plenty of other things to pray about.

Prayer that is personal, loving of God and all men, humble, filled with trust, eager for forgiveness, open to the movements of the Holy Spirit, and above all persevering, can do wonders—the very signs and wonders spoken of in the Bible itself.

James Keller

PRAYER FOR ACCEPTANCE

Sometimes I find it hard to realize
that You are a loving father, Lord.
Someone close to me dies or becomes seriously ill.
A senseless tragedy occurs—
an earthquake, a flood, a freak accident.
Children starve.
The poor and the aged are ignored.
People are hated because of their color
beliefs or birthplace.
When these things happen, I want to know why, Lord.
But You never answer.
And I, in the darkness of faith and trust in You
can only accept.
It's a lot like the way parents must treat young
children.
You don't explain fire or pain to a toddler.
You simply keep the ch`ld from touching the stove.
From my limited point of view, I can't hope
to understand the enormous mysteries of life.
I can try to approach them with love and compassion.
I can try to lessen, at least a little
the pain and suffering about me.
Amen.

FOR THE AGED

They have come a long way
Lord
and their journey
is just beginning.
They've had their taste
of happiness
and sorrow too.
They have made friends
and, sadly, a few enemies.
Success here
failure there.
But they did try.
They said they were sorry
for some things that happened.
I believe them.
More important, You do too.
Be a merciful Father
when You call them home.
Amen.

PRAYER FOR BROTHERHOOD

Father
You have made us.
Red, yellow, brown, white and black
tall and short, fat and thin
rich and poor, young and old—
all are Your children.
Teach us to cooperate rather than to compete
to respect rather than to revile
to forgive rather than condemn.
Your Son turned from no one.
May we learn, like Him, to be open
to the share of the divine
that You have implanted
in each of Your sons and daughters.
And may we forge a bond of love
that will make a living reality
the brotherhood in which we profess to believe.
Amen.

FOR BUSINESSMEN

Grant to those who engage
in commerce of any kind
Lord
to keep the public interest
ever in mind
with truthful advertising
trustworthy products
and honest practices.
Amen.

CHRISTOPHER PRAYER

Father, grant that I may be
a bearer of Christ Jesus, Your Son.
Allow me to warm the often cold, impersonal
scene of modern life with Your burning love.
Strengthen me, by Your Holy Spirit
to carry out my mission of changing the world
or some definite part of it, for the better.
Despite my lamentable failures, bring home to me
that my advantages are Your blessings
to be shared with others.
Make me more energetic in setting to rights
what I find wrong with the world
instead of complaining about it or myself.
Nourish in me a practical desire
to build up rather than tear down
to reconcile more than polarize
to go out on a limb rather than crave security.
Never let me forget that it is far better
to light one candle than to curse the darkness.
And to join my light, one day, with Yours.
Amen.

FOR CITIES

Cities are for needs and wants
divine Father
that cannot be met in isolation.
Have we expected from them too much
and put in too little?
Spur us to renew our cities
as You renew the earth in spring
that families may have decent living space
that the poor may have hope fulfilled
that the sick and aged
may be treated as persons.
May our cities
be filled with love
truly homes and not merely structures.
Amen.

FOR CIVIL AUTHORITY

If Your power
flows to public servants
through us the people
shouldn't our bitter complaints
lead us to self-scrutiny—
and action?
Amen.

PRAYER TO COPE WITH ANGER

Lord
sometimes I get angry, really mad.
And I say or do things
that I later regret.
Then I apologize for the cutting remark
the cruel accusation.
But apologies aren't always enough.
There may be no way to undo the harm.
Help me to accept my temper as a reality.
Help me to control it and direct it
into constructive channels.
Help me to harness my anger
so that it will move me to work to
relieve the oppression of the poor
the needless slaughter around the globe
the destruction of earth's beauties.
Above all, help me to learn restraint.
For a moment's hesitation can mean
preventing a lifetime of regret.
Amen.

PRAYER FOR COURAGE

When tensions build up on the job
and pressures at home begin to mount
and life becomes almost too much to bear
I sometimes get scared, Lord.
I get the urge to run away and hide
like the young man in the garden who fled
when the police came to arrest You.
How is it that You stood Your ground
and did not back off from Your teaching?
A little while before, You sweated blood
but You found strength to yield
to the Father's will
and draw power from it.
The next time I waver
or grow faint-hearted
help me to stand firm.
And having found the source of strength—
to reach out to others
who may be just as scared as I.
Amen.

A PRAYER ABOUT DEATH

Father
I don't want to die.
I don't even like to think about it.
But death is inevitable.
And every death, near and far
reminds me of my own.
Will it be the end of everything I know?
The final severance from those I love?
The total interruption of works
that are important to me?
What I can't seem to get into my head
is that death is part of life.
Otherwise You wouldn't let it happen
to Your Son—or to me.
Give me, please
a new kind of vision
a fresh burst of energy
to let myself go when the time comes.
To see the end as a beginning
the parting as a reunion
the last curtain as the lifting of a veil.
Amen.

PRAYER IN MOMENTS OF DESPAIR

God
sometimes I just want to give up
stop dead in my tracks
go off someplace and hide.
I get so tired and don't want to try any more.
Where can I find the courage and strength to go on?
The hope that things will eventually get better
isn't enough.
The thought that adversity builds character
doesn't convince me.
The only thing that gives me any hope is the
example of Your Son.
He didn't quit even though He faced death
which He conquered in His resurrection.
May what He did teach me.
May I find in His life the pattern
according to which I can live mine.
And may I try—at least in a small way—to urge
others to keep trying even though they feel they've
come up against a dead end.
Amen.

AN EASTER PRAYER

"He is risen"
That through Him we may rediscover faith:
in ourselves
in our world
in our God.
"He is risen"
That in Him we may rekindle hope:
for the abandoned
for the despairing
for the dreamless.
"He is risen"
That with Him we may restore love:
to those from whom we have kept it
to those who are most near us
to those we will never meet—
to all and everything.
"He is risen."
Amen.

FOR FAITH

A few years ago
Some men were saying
that You were dead.
Some still claim they can't be sure
or can't be bothered.
Some are torn and wracked with doubt.
Some of us who believe
aren't a very good proof
of Your compassion for humanity.
Let us show it more
so that Your praises may be sung
on every continent and far-off island.
Amen.

A PRAYER FOR FAITH

A few things still need to be set straight
Lord.
A few important relationships
like Yours and mine.
When I was a child I had faith
nothing great, but it was simple and strong.
The years may not have brought wisdom
but some growth and much perplexity.
Doing things my way has left me
half pleased
but hungry for inner peace.
Maybe it wasn't You I was rejecting
but dry formulas on a printed page
that I didn't really understand.
If You're willing to try again
so am I—and this time
You may find that I'm a little
more ready for an open-ended involvement
that goes by the name of—faith.
Amen.

PRAYER FOR ONE'S FAMILY

Father
sometimes the family
gets me down.
The children are noisy
and bills pile up.
Relatives and friends make demands
on my time and attention.
I try to keep first things first
and create an atmosphere where Your name
is honored, Your word observed.
But I get tired
and a hard edge creeps into my voice.
Help me to cope with the daily strains
of living in a family.
Help me to sustain a climate in which
my partner can grow in Your love
to encourage my children to develop fully
the talents You have given them
and to make of my family
the community of love
that Your Son came to bring.
Amen.

PRAYER FOR FORGIVENESS

Father
how weak we are
is not exactly news to You.
Every day in many ways
we start out with marvelous intentions
and end up trying to get even
to get out of responsibility
to nurture dishonesty in thought or act.
Forgive us, Lord.
Your Son knew us well
and we know not what we do.
Even more, let us have some of Your power
so that we may forgive one another.
That's where most of our trouble starts.
And, on a deeper level
help us forgive ourselves
to believe in Your pardon
gained by dying and rising.
Forgiveness instead of resentment
could get to be a habit—and not a bad one at that.
Amen.

PRAYER ON FRIENDSHIP

God
why is it so hard to get close to people
to let people get close to me
to make friends?
Is it because I've been hurt before
and am afraid to be vulnerable again?
Is it because I think
others will take advantage of my openness?
Your Son had twelve close friends.
One sold Him for thirty pieces of silver.
Another denied that he ever knew Him.
The rest ran away when He needed them most.
Jesus even predicted these things
—yet He didn't shut Himself off from friendship.
Make me willing to take the risk, too.
Help me to realize that, ultimately, in opening
to another human being
we are opening ourselves to You.
Amen.

PRAYER FOR GOD'S GOOD EARTH

Father
the Bible tells us
You looked on all that You made
and saw that it was good.
But we have been too willing
to squander the richness of creation.
We have laid the ax to the mighty forests
despoiled the green hillsides
wasted earth's mineral wealth.
We have fouled the air
littered the countryside
and polluted the streams and oceans.
Voices are raised
to stop us from squandering our patrimony.
May we heed them in time so that one day
we can look on the planet you have given us
and say with pride, once again
"Behold, it is good."
Amen.

A PRAYER FOR GOVERNMENT

Father
a handful of courageous men
in a moment of danger
pledged their lives, fortunes and honor
to proclaim a nation whose citizens' rights
were based, not upon the nod of king or ruler
but upon creation at Your hands.
Grant to our administration
a ministry of service to all, not the few.
To our Congress, the upholding of public interest
not merely a welter of competing private claims.
To our judiciary, a wisdom in interpreting law
grounded in principle, not expediency.
Pour Your Spirit out upon our people
so that they may become active
in the affairs of government
that they may not confuse dissent for disloyalty
that they may use their mighty power
for the healing of differences among nations
with justice and mercy and love.
Amen.

PRAYER FOR GROWTH IN LOVE

Father
You have loved us from eternity
without conditions.
Whether we are beautiful or plain
rich or poor
saintly or sinful
makes no difference.
Why can't we be that way toward each other?
Why do we magnify each other's shortcomings
and ignore the good features?
Help us to grow in love as Your Son did—
a love that doesn't gloss over failings
but one that accepts them and then goes
on to stress what is good in all we meet
what can be built on to help the other person
become fully himself or herself.
Then, Lord, as we increase our
ability to love as Jesus did
we will come closer
to the kingdom He preached.
Amen.

PRAYER FOR THE HANDICAPPED

Hear our prayer, O Lord, for the handicapped.
Bless them in their trials.
They bear a visible cross
one that is often overlooked, slighted
ignored, avoided.
They must bear a heavy burden.
Yet they face the same problems as others
without the same strength and resources.
Protect them from harm and hurt.
Bolster their confidence and strength.
Help them to find satisfaction
in what they can do.
Make those who can ease their burden
eager to do so.
Make those who can share their trial
willing to do so.
Make those of us who do not share their limitations
aware of how much more we can do with the talents
You have entrusted to our keeping.
Amen.

PRAYER FOR HONESTY

God
it's hard to be honest
to know what my real intentions are
to admit my true motives.
And it's so easy to use "white lies"
to get out of sticky situations
to tell a half-truth to avoid embarrassment
or inconvenience.
I excuse myself by thinking I'm honest
when I'm only being tactless or sarcastic.
That doesn't prevent me from assigning to others
motives that are less noble.
Teach me to face the discomfort of knowing myself
and to give others the benefit of the doubt.
Make me tireless in seeking to do Your will
which in my heart I recognize
more than I care to admit.
Weakness, slowness and mistakes
are part of the human scene.
Make me honest enough to treat the inadequacies of
other people the way I would want them—and You—
to deal with mine.
Amen.

FOR HOPE

You once told the prophet Isaiah
that those who hoped in You
would have the wings of eagles.
Things are getting me down, Lord.
I need those wings
and I'm not the only one.
With them, I can never completely fall
and the world stands to gain
by the perseverance I urgently seek.
Amen.

PRAYER FOR HUSBANDS AND WIVES

Lord, inspire those men and women
who bear the titles "Husband" and "Wife."
Help them to look to You
to themselves
to one another
to rediscover the fullness and mystery
they once felt in their union.
Let them be honest enough to ask:
"Where have we been together
and where are we going?"
Let them be brave enough to question:
"How have we failed?"
Let each be foolhardy enough to say:
"For me, we come first."
Help them, together
to reexamine their commitment
in the light of Your love—
willingly, openly, compassionately.
Help them, together
to believe how fragile, yet powerful—
how weak, yet how strong—
how impossible, yet attainable
their love can be.
Give "Husband" and "Wife" the courage
to be for each other a person
rather than a title.
Amen.

FOR LABORERS

Your Son was a carpenter
Father.
But some people look down on
those who work with their hands.
Inspire those in offices and factories
on farms and in machine shops
to put heart into what they do
to take pride in their strength
and the products of their toil.
They couldn't have a better example.
Amen.

PRAYER FOR LEADERS

Jesus
You said that anyone who wants to be a leader
must learn to be everyone's servant.
I find that hard to accept.
Sometimes I'd like to be a public official
have a limousine and a staff of assistants.
Or I'd like to be famous and get VIP treatment
in restaurants, hotels and airports.
I'd like to be a champion athlete
win trophies, sign autographs
and hold world's records.
At such times I don't want
to be anyone's servant.
Teach me
why You became everyone's servant.
Teach me why the truly great leaders—
those who accomplished the greatest good for
the largest number of people—
were men and women who knew that to lead is to serve.
Motivate me to begin leading those I meet daily
by discovering their needs
and striving to help them live up to their potential.
Amen.

PRAYER TO BE A BETTER LISTENER

We don't really listen to each other, God.
At least not all the time.
Instead of true dialogue, we carry on
two parallel monologues.
I talk.
My companion talks.
But what we're really concentrating on is
how to sound good
how to make our points strongly
how to outshine the person we're talking with.
Teach us to listen as Your Son listened
to everyone who spoke with Him.
Remind us that, somehow, You are trying
to reach us through our partner
in conversation.
Your truth, Your love, Your goodness are
seeking us out in the truth, love and goodness
being communicated.
When our words are harsh, hostile, angry
we convey the very opposite of those qualities.
Teach us to be still, Lord
that we may truly hear our brothers and sisters—
and, in them, You.
Amen.

PRAYER TO LIVE IN THE PRESENT

God
I spend so much time reliving yesterday
or anticipating tomorrow
that I lose sight of the only time
that is really mine—the present.
Remind me that the past—with its successes
and failures—is over.
I can make amends where I have hurt others
or let them down
But I can't undo what has been done.
The future is yet to be
and eagerness or apprehension
will not hasten it—or postpone it.
You give me today, one minute at a time.
That's all I have—all I ever will.
Give me the faith that knows that each moment
contains exactly what is best for me.
Give me the hope that trusts You enough to
forget past sins and future trials.
Give me the love that makes each minute of
life an anticipation of eternity with You.
Amen.

FOR THE LONELY

It's awful to be lonely, Lord.
Sometimes
when I'm in a crowded room
surrounded by people who love me
I still feel lonely.
I'll bet the world is full
of lonely people
sitting on park benches
and bar stools
in movie theaters
and at cocktail parties.
My next-door neighbor
has never knocked on my door.
Why is that, Lord?
Help your lonely, Lord
to reach out of themselves.
If only we weren't so afraid
of being hurt in the process . . .
We'd really like
to become more aware of
and responsive to one another.
Grant us strength
to take the risk involved . . .
The hurt can't be worse
than this awful lonely feeling.
Help us, Lord
to overcome our loneliness
by becoming one
with each other
and one with You.
Amen.

PRAYER IN TIME OF MENTAL ANGUISH

God
sometimes I think physical pain is less hard
to bear than mental suffering.
A toothache or a broken leg
is at least in one place.
But anxiety or tension
guilt or indecision
is everywhere at once—and nowhere.
When Jesus said, "Not my will but Yours be done,"
did His pain go away?
I don't think so.
But I do believe that You
made it possible for Him to bear it.
Do for me, Father, whatever it was
You did for Him.
As I try to imitate His fidelity to Your will
may I experience Your peace—
the peace that, somehow, can exist in the
midst of great suffering.
Amen.

PRAYER FOR THOSE
WITH MONEY PROBLEMS

Father
Your Son told us to consider
the lilies of the field.
But it's hard not to worry
when the rent comes due
just at income tax time.
The antics of an 8-year-old
add to the doctor bills
and a teenager breaks a tooth.
The old car is falling apart
and how will the kids get to school
without another one?
Teach me to use my income responsibly.
Show me how to share
what has been given me
with those who have a lot less.
Drive home to me what Jesus meant
when He said to lay up treasures
where neither rust nor moth consumes.
Amen.

FOR NEIGHBORS

Help me to understand the answer
Jesus gave to the question:
"Who is my neighbor?"
About a man on a road who needed help
about those who refused it
and the one person who gave it.
Make me more sensitive
to the feelings of those I meet
at home, in a store, on a bus, in a crowd.
More aware
that whether I know them or not—
the nameless, the angry, the anguished
all people, everywhere
are my neighbors in You.
No one is really a stranger
unless I choose to make him so.
Amen.

PRAYER FOR OPENNESS

Lord
help me to see
the plight of those around me
the conditions in which my brothers live.
Lord
help me to hear
the cry of the anguished
the whisper of the hopeless
the plea of the forgotten.
Lord
help me recognize the stench of poverty
the odor of illness
the air of loneliness.
Lord
help me to realize
why some people have no taste for life
no palate for living.
Lord
help me to reach out and touch
these my brothers
with humility, reverence and love.
Amen.

FOR PARENTS

Heavenly Father
You have given to men and women
the awesome opportunity
to participate in the creation of life
to nurture their children
to teach them the values and skills
they will need as responsible
creative adults.
Bless fathers and mothers
as they take on the joys and sorrows
of parenthood.
Enlighten them to communicate
an awareness of those things
that truly count.
Strengthen them when they falter.
Deepen their love for one another
no less than for their children.
Their love must know how to sacrifice
how to absorb friction and conflict.
Their love is something special
because it speaks, however haltingly
of Yours.
Amen.

PRAYER FOR PATIENCE

Lord
do I need patience!
I want to get things done.
There are too many slums
too much hypocrisy, too many words
too little flow from thought to act.
I see it in others, I see it in myself.
Is it any wonder that in my better moments
frustration leads to impatience.
Only, it doesn't work that way, does it?
What am I getting uptight about
when it all depends on You?
Teach me to sit still, to think, to pray
so that when there is something to do
I may do it with clear sight,
with energy, with effectiveness
and maybe with a little
more love
than I have been showing myself or anybody else.
Amen.

FOR PEACE

From the deserts of Sinai
to the swamps of Indo-China
men give their lips to peace
and their hands to war.
Nothing proves
man's radical wound
and need for Your Presence
like brother against brother.
Peace, like her sister Justice
requires the vision, discipline
and love
that only You can give.
Give.
This time may we be ready.
Amen.

FOR PERSEVERANCE

Guide and strengthen me
Holy Spirit
in trying to accomplish
the mission in life
You have assigned to me.
You haven't exactly made it easy.
But when I think
of Abraham, and Moses, and Paul
I stop complaining.
I want to honor You
do some good for a lot of people
and then rest—with You—
for a long time.
Amen.

PRAYER FOR PERSONAL GROWTH

God
what makes it so difficult to get rid of
things I don't like about myself?
I can't stop smoking—or maybe it's drinking
or pills or overeating.
My short temper really bothers me
but I can't seem to change it.
I keep thinking that underneath all the
self-indulgence, sloth and meanness
there's a person I'd really like to be—
that others would like too.
What keeps me from becoming that person?
Father, help me to know myself—
what I am and can become.
Enable me to see the good in myself and rejoice in it
to see flaws and change them.
Teach me to live with myself, to accept myself
mindful that becoming what You want me to be
is more like cultivating a garden
than chopping down a forest.
Amen.

FOR THE POOR AND HUNGRY

Father
it's easy to forget
the poor, the hungry, the cold, the sick.
I have a warm coat, a comfortable home
running water, a nearby supermarket
a regular job.
What I have
is not mine
without strings.
But if I can only remember
that the strings
are lines of love
it won't be so hard
to share
my time, my attention, my respect
with those You love
(as if You didn't love everybody!).
And get back
without seeking it
a new appreciation
of the dignity
of those who suffer.
Your blessings are not inert.
If we let them
they spring us into action.
Amen.

A PRAYER OF PRAISE

Praise to You, Father
for the innocent eyes of children
for sunlight and flowers and snowfalls
for the muscles of men who build houses
and hospitals and harbors
for the minds of scholars
who unfold the truths of the universe
for the hearts of parents who teach us to love.
We praise You for what we have.
We praise You, too, for those things
that Your wise love has decided
to withhold from us.
What we are and have is from You.
And our grateful response can only be
to share these treasures
with all Your children.
And praise to You, too, Father
for so many brothers and sisters.
Amen.

PRAYER FOR A SENSE OF HUMOR

It was pretty funny
Lord
I have to admit.
But does the laughter
always have to be at my expense?
I'm not the only one
who uses the wrong word
or gets caught in an absurd situation.
I turn out to be the butt
of everyone else's joke
—more so lately.
Or does it only seem that way?
Am I getting too touchy
too quick to defend myself
against anything that would make me—
well, like the rest of humanity, I guess.
Next time, help me to see
the humor in the situation
and not imagine that people's merriment
is prompted by unkindness.
After all, I am a bit foolish at times
and I suppose I had it coming.
Amen.

PRAYER FOR TEACHERS

Lord, it helps me to remember
that You were a teacher.
You were a lot of other things
but there is something very human
and reassuring
in Your giving the word of life
to restless, uncertain people.
You never used a chalkboard
corrected exams
or sat through a graduation ceremony.
But You rejoiced with men and women
and little children
who discovered for the first time
what it means to be sons and daughters
of a good Father.
Grant a full measure of Your Spirit
to those whose task it is
to awaken minds and hearts
to the wonders of creation
the insights of science
the relation of cause and effect.
They often get discouraged, Lord.
Lift them up by Your example and power.
Amen.

A PRAYER OF THANKS

Thank you, God, for hot water
for windows that let in the air
and keep out the cold.
For gas and electric at the
flick of a wrist.
For the comfort that greets me as I
open the door from the windy night.
Bless those who find no warmth
on the streets, in condemned buildings
in fellow-sufferers, in passersby.
Let Your blessing be shown
in my regard for the lonely man
on the park bench
the frightened and bewildered teenage drug-taker
the family whose color is different.
Let me know too
that in sharing what I have and am
with those who are in need
I am doing nothing especially noble—
only what You expect by way of thanks.
Amen.

FOR THANKSGIVING

For the sparkle in the eyes
of loved ones
for the touch of a friendly hand
for the bread we eat
for the plentiful stars
for the roar of the breakers
for the Holy Word
You have spoken to us
for the chance to be
and to do
we thank You
O Lord, our God.
Amen.

PRAYER FOR UNDERSTANDING

Lord
it's so easy to jump to conclusions
and make
snap judgments
to fix permanent labels on people
because of a few words they've said
a single action they've done.
But You created us
as beings capable of change
able to correct our defects
redeemable.
Help us to see one another
as You have made us.
Help us to understand
that anyone can fail
but also that anyone
can rise from failure.
Help us to give others—and ourselves—
the benefit of the doubt.
Amen.

FOR UNITY

We were one
at the start
and now
we are many.
Not just
the many
of diversity
but the many
of division too.
Truth is one.
You are one.
Why can't
we be one?
And know
in You
the unity
of love?
Amen.

PRAYER FOR WORLD VISION

When I turn off the 11 o'clock news
I glance at my watch
and yawn, and it's off to bed.
Nothing wrong with that.
But what of those babies
crying motherless outside the
Vietnamese village?
The vacant stare of the Appalachian coal miner
with only memories of a job?
The men and women in the sweatshops of Hong Kong
the prison camps of Siberia
the resettlement areas of South Africa
the prisons of Brazil—
they are all part of my family.
How will they sleep tonight?
Let me use
what little voice and power I have
to speak and act on their behalf.
For we have but one world, Lord
or none at all.
Amen.

FOR WRITERS

Writing is a lonely business, Lord.
A writer sits at a typewriter
or with pen in hand—
and often the page remains blank.
Touch their fingertips
and jog their brains
with a spark of Your creative power.
Gently direct them
to communicate more for truth than profit
to give us the highest aspirations
of the human spirit
while not flinching from our tragic flaws.
Help them
to share with us
moments of adventure
instants of joy
hours of reflection.
Don't let them down, Lord
or let them disappoint You.
In print, or on the stage, or on the airwaves
their words shape our very lives
images or distortions
of the Word that was
"in the beginning."
Amen.

FOR YOUTH

The young need someone
to listen to them
Lord.
Open my ears that much wider
so that by talking to me
they may be more willing
to listen to You.
Grant them
confidence and guidance
where they have a right
to expect it.
I really want their world
to be better than mine.
Amen.